Exploring Planets
MARS

Michelle Lomberg

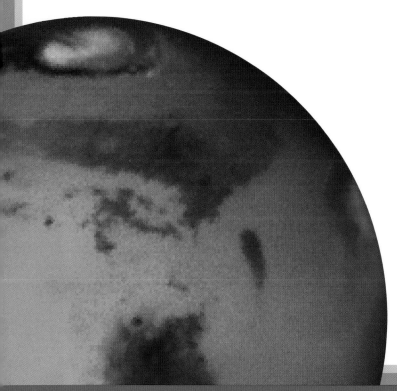

WEIGL PUBLISHERS INC.

Published by Weigl Publishers Inc.
350 5th Avenue, Suite 3304, PMB 6G
New York, NY USA 10118-0069
Web site: www.weigl.com
Copyright 2004 WEIGL PUBLISHERS INC.

Library of Congress Cataloging-in-Publication Data

Lomberg, Michelle.
  Mars / Michelle Lomberg.
     v. cm. -- (Exploring planets)
Includes index.
Contents: Introducing Mars -- What's in a name? -- Mars spotting --
Early observations -- Mars in the solar system -- Mars and Earth --
Missions to Mars -- Mars explorer: Bob Mase -- Mars explorer: Giovanni
Schiaparelli -- Mars on the web -- Activity: Mars math-- What have you
learned?
  ISBN 1-59036-099-0 (lib. bdg. : alk. paper) – ISBN 1-59036-226-8 (pbk.)
  1. Mars (Planet)--Juvenile literature. [1. Mars (Planet)] I. Title.
II. Series.
  QB641 .L66 2003
  523.43--dc21
                              2002014495

Printed in the United States of America
1 2 3 4 5 6 7 8 9 0 08 07 06 05 04

Photograph Credits
Every reasonable effort has been made to trace ownership and to obtain permission to reprint
copyright material. The publishers would be pleased to have any errors or omissions brought
to their attention so that they may be corrected in subsequent printings.

Cover: Photos.com (top); Digital Vision (bottom)

Virginia Boulay: page 12; **CORBIS/MAGMA:** pages 6 (Araldo de Luca), 11 (Tom Bean), 17 (AFP);
Corel Corporation: page 19; **Digital Vision:** page 22; **EyeWire, Inc.:** page 21; **Calvin J. Hamilton:**
page 7R; **Hulton|Archive by Getty Images:** pages 10, 18R; **JPL/TSADO/Tom Stack & Associates:**
page 7L; **NASA:** pages 1, 4, 8, 9, 13, 14, 16, 18L.

Project Coordinator Jennifer Nault **Design** Terry Paulhus **Copy Editor** Kara Turner
Layout Virginia Boulay **Photo Researcher** Tina Schwartzenberger

Contents

Introducing Mars 4

Name That Planet 6

Mars Spotting 8

Early Observations 10

Mars in Our Solar System 12

Mars and Earth 14

Missions to Mars 16

Planet People 18

Mars on the Internet 20

Young Scientists at Work 21

What Have You Learned? 22

Words to Know/Index 24

Introducing Mars

Mars is one of the nine planets in our **solar system**. It is the fourth planet from the Sun. Sky watchers have observed this planet since ancient times. Mars has been the subject of **myths** and stories for thousands of years. People still make movies about Mars today. Read on to learn about this fascinating planet.

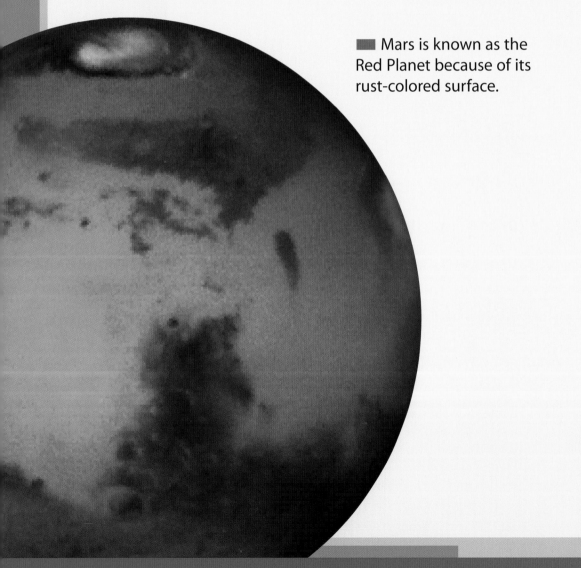

Mars is known as the Red Planet because of its rust-colored surface.

Mars Facts

- Mars makes an **orbit** around the Sun once every 678 days.

- The north and south poles of Mars are covered in **dry ice**.

- Dust storms are common on Mars. Some storms last for months.

- Scientists think that Mars had water on its surface billions of years ago.

- Mars's two moons are not round. They are lumpy and look like potatoes.

- Olympus Mons is a mountain on Mars. It is the highest mountain in our solar system.

- There are no Martians on Mars. Still, the word "Martian" is used to describe things on Mars.

Name That Planet

Mars is named after the Roman god of war. Ancient Romans thought that the planet Mars was the color of blood.

Astronomers in India also thought the planet was the color of blood. They named Mars *Mangala*. It is linked to the Hindu war god *Kartikeya*. Chinese astronomers noticed Mars's bright color, too. The Chinese name for Mars means "fire."

The Greek name for the god of war is Ares.

Martian Moons

Mars's two moons are very small and lumpy. Each moon is about the size of a small town.

The Greek god of war had two dogs. They were named Deimos and Phobos. *Deimos* means "panic," and *Phobos* means "fear." Mars's two moons are also called Deimos and Phobos.

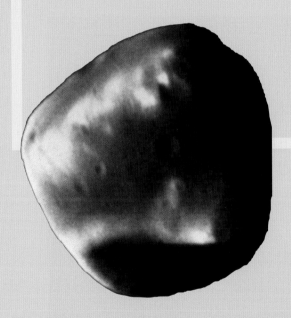

Deimos

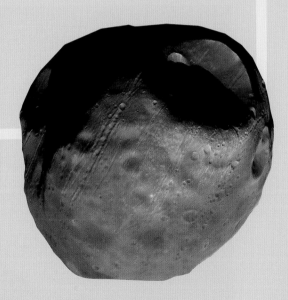

Phobos

Mars Spotting

Mars is about 50 million miles (80.5 million kilometers) from Earth. This distance changes because Mars's orbit is not a perfect circle. Mars is sometimes 35 million miles (56.3 million km) from Earth.

Every 2 years, Earth passes between the Sun and Mars. This is called a Mars opposition. Mars is very bright in the sky during an opposition. The planet can be seen all night.

■ Earth's mass is 10 times the mass of Mars. An object's mass is its size and bulk.

See for Yourself

You do not need a powerful **telescope** to see Mars in the night sky. Mars looks like a bright red star. Unlike a star, Mars does not stay in one place. It travels across the sky in its orbit. In North America, Mars can usually be spotted in September. Science center staff can tell you where to look for Mars in the night sky.

■ Mars appears red owing to its iron-rich soil.

Early Observations

People have known about Mars since ancient times. Egyptian astronomers recorded their sightings of Mars long ago.

Mars was mapped in the 1500s. Danish astronomer Tycho Brahe used math to find Mars's position in the sky.

Astronomer Asaph Hall worked for the United States Naval Observatory. He discovered Mars's two moons in 1877.

Tycho Brahe calculated Mars's position in the sky before the telescope was invented.

Cracks on Mars

Astronomer Percival Lowell was born in Boston in 1855. In 1894, Percival built the Lowell Observatory in Arizona. He studied the sky's objects from the observatory. He took special notice of Mars. Percival believed that the cracks on Mars were unusual. He thought they proved that there had been life on Mars.

Astronomers continue to study space at the Lowell Observatory.

Mars in Our Solar System

Mars is one of the nine planets in our solar system. It is the fourth planet from the Sun.

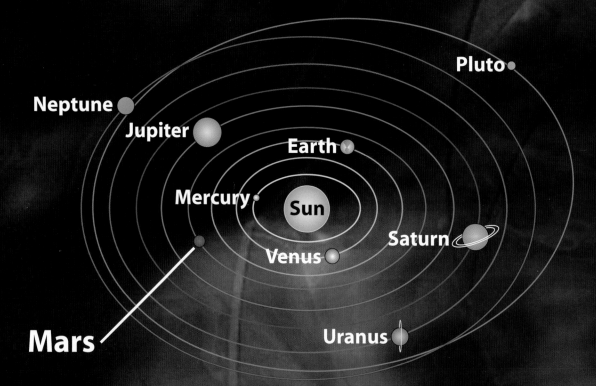

Pluto

Neptune

Jupiter

Earth

Mercury

Sun

Saturn

Venus

Mars

Uranus

Mars has polar icecaps. Their size and shape changes over time.

Mars has long cracks on its surface. These cracks look like dried-up riverbeds. Some scientists believe that Mars once had water on it.

Mars and Earth

Mars and Earth have many common features. Like Earth, Mars has mountains and icecaps. Still, Mars is much colder than Earth. Mars's air would poison humans. People could not live on Mars without protective spacesuits. Some astronomers believe that Mars was once more like Earth. They think that the planet lost its **atmosphere** over millions of years.

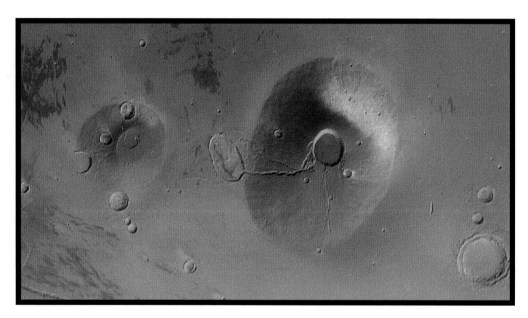

■ The surface of Mars has canyons and volcanoes. Some of the lava flows are still visible around the planet's older volcanoes.

Compare the Planets

PLANET FEATURES					
PLANET	**Distance from the Sun**	**Days to Orbit the Sun**	**Diameter**	**Length of Day**	**Average Temperature**
Mercury	36 million miles (58 million km)	88	3,032 miles (4,880 km)	4,223 hours	333° Fahrenheit (167° C)
Venus	67 million miles (108 million km)	225	7,521 miles (12,104 km)	2,802 hours	867° Fahrenheit (464° C)
Earth	93 million miles (150 million km)	365	7,926 miles (12,756 km)	24 hours	59° Fahrenheit (15° C)
Mars	142 million miles (229 million km)	687	4,222 miles (6,975 km)	25 hours	−81° Fahrenheit (−63° C)
Jupiter	484 million miles (779 million km)	4,331	88,846 miles (142,984 km)	10 hours	−230° Fahrenheit (−146° C)
Saturn	891 million miles (1,434 million km)	10,747	74,897 miles (120,535 km)	11 hours	−285° Fahrenheit (−176° C)
Uranus	1,785 million miles (2,873 million km)	30,589	31,763 miles (51,118 km)	17 hours	−355° Fahrenheit (−215° C)
Neptune	2,793 million miles (4,495 million km)	59,800	30,775 miles (49,528 km)	16 hours	−355° Fahrenheit (−215° C)
Pluto	3,647 million miles (5,869 million km)	90,588	1,485 miles (2,390 km)	153 hours	−375° Fahrenheit (−226° C)

Missions to Mars

Astronomers have sent **space probes** to orbit and land on Mars. Space probes gather information about objects in space. The *Mars Pathfinder* is a space probe. It landed on Mars in 1997. The *Mars Pathfinder* was carrying a **rover** called *Sojourner*.

■ *Sojourner* moved around the surface of Mars on wheels.

U.S. MISSIONS TO MARS			
Space Probe	**Launched**	**Purpose**	**Results**
Mariner 4	1964	flyby	Took 21 photographs
Mariner 6	1969	flyby	Took 75 photographs
Mariner 7	1969	flyby	Took 126 photographs
Mariner 9	1971	orbiter	Took 7,329 photographs
Viking (1, 2)	1975	orbiter/lander	Took 50,000 photographs

Life on Mars?

Mars is sometimes struck by **asteroids**. When this happens, chunks of the planet are sent flying out into space. Some of these rocks reach Earth. These pieces are called meteorites when they land on Earth. Scientists discovered tiny grooves on one of these meteorites. These grooves appear to be **fossils** of small life forms. This could mean that Mars had life billions of years ago.

■ Scientists believe that fossils found on this rock are more than 3.5 billion years old.

Planet People

Giovanni Schiaparelli

Name: Giovanni Schiaparelli
Mars Accomplishments:
Discovered cracks on the surface of Mars

Giovanni Schiaparelli was born in 1835. This Italian astronomer studied the planet Mars. Giovanni saw long cracks on Mars's surface. He called these lines *canali*. This word means "channels" in Italian. People thought that Giovanni had discovered water canals like those built by humans. A strange idea began to spread. Some people thought that space aliens had built the canals.

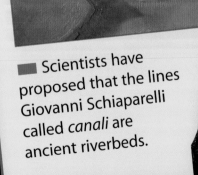
Scientists have proposed that the lines Giovanni Schiaparelli called *canali* are ancient riverbeds.

Bob Mase

Name: Bob Mase
Mars Accomplishments:
Guides Mars space probe

Bob Mase works at NASA. He is the head **space navigator** of the space probe *Mars Odyssey*. Bob works with a team of NASA scientists. Together, they guide the space probe in its orbit around Mars.

Bob grew up in Florida. His childhood home was not far from NASA's Kennedy Space Center. This made him interested in space at a young age.

When Bob Mase was a young boy, he could watch space shuttle launches from his backyard.

Mars on the Internet

To learn more about Mars, look for books at your school library. The Internet is also an excellent place to learn about Mars. There are many great Web sites with information. Just type the words *Mars* and *planet* into a search engine. Google and Yahoo are useful search engines.

The Internet has information on all of the planets in our solar system. To learn about the nine planets, visit these Web sites:

Encarta Homepage
www.encarta.com
Type the name of a planet that you would like to learn about into the search engine.

NASA Kids
http://kids.msfc.nasa.gov
NASA built a Web site for young learners just like you. Visit this site to learn more about the nine planets, space travel, and the latest NASA news.

Young Scientists at Work

Calculate Your Weight on Mars

Would you weigh the same on Mars as you do on Earth? No, you would not. Your weight depends on the gravity of the planet you are on. Gravity is the force that pulls you toward a planet's center. Mars has less gravity than Earth does. This means that you would weigh less on Mars.

To calculate your weight on Mars, multiply your Earth weight by 0.4.

(Your weight) x 0.4 = _____

What Have You Learned?

How much do you know about Mars?
Test your knowledge!

1 Why is Mars called the Red Planet?

2 Where does the name *Mars* come from?

3 Name the moons of Mars.

4 Can you see Mars without a telescope?

5 True or False? Mars was discovered in the 1500s.

6 Is it possible for people to live on Mars?

7 Did Martians build canals on Mars?

8 What did Giovanni Schiaparelli call the lines on the surface of Mars?

9 Which planet is closest to the Sun: Earth or Mars?

10 Which planet is larger: Earth or Mars?

What was your score?

9–10	You should work for NASA!
5–8	You are a good planet watcher!
0–4	You need to polish your telescope!

Answers

1 Mars is called the Red Planet because of its rust-colored surface. **2** Mars is named after the Roman god of war. **3** Deimos and Phobos **4** Yes, you can see Mars without a telescope. **5** False. People have known about Mars for thousands of years. **6** No, it is not possible for people to live on Mars. **7** No **8** *canali* **9** Earth is closer to the Sun than Mars. Earth is the third planet from the Sun, and Mars is the fourth planet from the Sun. **10** Earth is about twice the size of Mars.

Words to Know

asteroids: small, solid objects in space that circle the Sun

astronomers: people who study space and its objects

atmosphere: the layer of gases surrounding a planet

dry ice: frozen carbon dioxide gas

fossils: remains of ancient life forms

myths: stories or legends, often about gods or heroes

orbit: the nearly circular path a space object makes around another object in space

rover: a robotic vehicle used to explore the surface of a planet

solar system: the Sun, the planets, and other objects that move around the Sun

space navigator: a person who directs the travel of a spacecraft

space probes: spacecraft used to gather information about space

telescope: an instrument that makes distant objects appear closer

Index

asteroids 17

Brahe, Tycho 10

Earth 8, 12, 14, 15, 17, 21

Hall, Asaph 10

Lowell, Percival 11

Mars Pathfinder 16

Mase, Bob 19

moons (Deimos and Phobos) 5, 7, 10

orbit 5, 8, 9, 15, 16, 19

Schiaparelli, Giovanni 18

space probes 16, 19

Sun 4, 5, 8, 12, 15